Real Life *Romance*

Real Life Romance

Everyday Wisdom on *Love*, *Sex*, and *Relationships*

by *Leah Garchik*

Illustrations by *Miguel Gallardo*

CHRONICLE BOOKS

SAN FRANCISCO

Text copyright © 2007 by Leah Garchik.

Illustrations copyright © 2007 by Miguel Gallardo.

Library of Congress Cataloging-in-Publication Data available.

ISBN: 978-0-8118-6025-3

Manufactured in China.

Designed by Meghan Eplett.

Distributed in Canada by Raincoast Books
9050 Shaughnessy Street
Vancouver, British Columbia V6P 6E5

10 9 8 7 6 5 4 3 2 1

Chronicle Books LLC
680 Second Street
San Francisco, California 94107

www.chroniclebooks.com

Introduction

Since the human race needs sex to continue its merry progression from generation to generation, and since love leads to sex and romance leads to love, **romance is a biological necessity.** It is also a popular pastime and the subject of much yammering. The speakers in this book, some of them hunting for love and others spectators of the sport, have told it like it *isn't*, like it *might be*, like it *should be*, like it *would have been*, AND like *if only it were*.

Readers of the *San Francisco Chronicle* submitted the overheard remarks for use in a daily column, the construction and maintenance of which is my job. ***They listened for comments in all sorts of public spaces,*** and, of course, special attention was paid if the quotes were dirty. Overhearing many conversations was facilitated by the speakers' use of cell phones. ***Quotes were submitted by all sorts of people on all sorts of subjects,*** including chores, astrology, baseball, and the price per pound of heritage tomatoes compared to the price of a gallon of gas.

But romance is the subject people most enjoy discussing. If we keep in mind its essential role—we'rc not talking about sales of perfumed stationery; we're talking about the propagation of the species—this makes sense.

The ideal romance starts with naïveté and optimism and moves from there to curiosity and enchantment, desire and passion, lust and satisfaction. Eventually, however, the lovers arrive at a fork in the road. One way leads to ennui and indifference, anger and disgust, revenge and despair, and, once again, solitude.

The other route—often a toll road—leads to shared appetizers, security, serenity, laughter, and a lifetime of enthusiastic sex (or, even if not, the bonanza of taking public transit together at a discounted rate).

All the while,
they just keep talking.

Getting Ready

The prelude to romance is often little more than a vague longing for the obscure. Personal qualifications are assessed, and within time, longing morphs into a desire for the specific.

"If I was a *dude,*
I'd date me."

*Young woman to man,
on ski lift.*

"You know,
he said I'm still
fertile."

*Woman to companion,
at fourth hole of golf course.*

"I don't want to go out and *screw* everyone that I meet. I just want to know that I can."

Advocate of empowerment, in coffee shop near campus.

17

"*All* the English majors I know are on *antidepressants.*"

Woman to fellow diners, at restaurant.

"I was going to wait until I got married to get a salad spinner."

Lettuce lover, downtown in city.

"My boss just announced that we are having a retreat after the first of the year. *I guess this means I'll have to buy some pajamas.*"

Woman to companion, in checkout line at drugstore.

"The only time I really miss having a man in my life is *garbage night*."

Trashy but particular woman,
in courthouse on Valentine's Day.

"What I need is a man who *will let me henpeck him*."

Picky female pedestrian,
in town known for feminism.

"I'm no longer looking for a mate. *I just want to have sex.*"

Famous choreographer to admiring members of civic club.

"You know, Bernard's son used to *play with farm animals.*"

Elderly woman to another, leaving the matinee of a play about a man who falls in love with a goat.

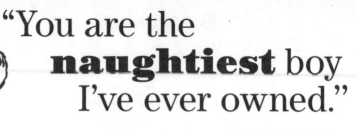

"You are the **naughtiest** boy I've ever owned."

Woman to dog, outside pet shelter.

> "I really am attracted to people with hyphenated names. *It shows extra effort.*"
>
> *Discriminating passenger, on shuttle bus between hospitals.*

> "Remember, girls love
> **eye patches and scars.**"
>
> *High school freshman boy advising eleven-year-old rookie, on bus.*

"Like I said,
I don't know what a kiss does."

One teenage boy to another, at rural county fair.

"Have you ever thought about
going natural? Because I am completely
natural now, and you know how
many men hit on me, Mom."

Young man on cell phone, in discount food mart.

"*I'd French-kiss a dog on its lips any time;* I don't care where it's been. Now, people, well, I won't necessarily shake their hands."

Server of snacks to customer, at coffeehouse.

"Rick still wants me to go out with this friend of his, the *nymphomaniac*. But to be honest, I don't have the time."

Young man to young man, on college campus.

"Well, *he is brilliant*, but those types of people are idiots."

Woman on cell phone, in town populated by many Nobel Prize winners.

"*Is he really a Jewish prince?*"
"That's what people say."
"Wow, he's everything else, and royalty, too."

Three teenage girls, around resort pool.

Getting Close

Both parties are available, close enough to make contact. But the planning and carrying-out of an introduction to a stranger can be delicate.

"For the love of God, just **Google him** and then you'll know."

Research recommendation,
in discount clothing store.

"He's attractive, he's nice, *and he has cows.*"

Young woman to another, in Texas.

"The only thing is, his

hair is kind of *weird*."

One coif connoisseur to another, on downtown corner.

"No, send me the
other bouquet,
***the one with the
obscene flowers.***"

*Woman on cell phone,
in suburb with palatial homes
and neat lawns.*

"I did something really pathetic last night."
"Did it involve *Craigslist*?"

Remorse-filled commuter and savvy friend,
on bus in hipster neighborhood.

"I knew she was in an *abusive relationship*, but I didn't know she played lacrosse."

Girl to girl, in high school restroom.

"Hey, I know you from an AA meeting. I remember your story of being in rehab."

One potential date to another, on public transportation.

"Well, you should have gotten her phone number while you could still write."

Man to wistful man, at harborside restaurant.

"I was looking for someone for just a really good time, but then I *peeked* at his iTunes playlist. He'd be serious baggage."

Music lover, in suburb with many Lexus drivers.

"Black leather jacket?
Sunglasses? Oh, my God!
I would have so done him
if I wasn't running to a final."

Female student to friend, in college café.

"With all due respect,

"Yeah, he's hot, but I could never do it with a guy with an American flag tattoo . . . unless he was straight."

Patriotic but particular woman, at '70s–themed disco party.

your fly is open."

Woman to man, on bus heading downtown.

"You're not ugly, but if you were smarter, you'd be hot."

Man attempting pickup, overheard by bartender.

"No, you don't know me, but we met last night, and **I'm in love with you."**

Man on cell phone, in delicatessen.

"I think you're very pretty, and we could have beautiful children. *And I won't stalk you when you break up with me."*

Man taking the long view, in business district.

"Do you want me to *hypnotize* you, or are we just going to talk?"

Man on cell phone, in airport.

"I'm not saying you are a *mental midget*. But you play checkers and I play chess."

Man to woman, at bar in upscale Greek restaurant.

"He asked if I wanted to go back to his place. That's the same as the old-fashioned *'Do you want to go for a cup of coffee?'*"

Young woman to another, on streetcar.

"You guys can go to Tommy's without me. His mom gets all **Demi Moore** on me."

High school student to his pals.

Getting Going

The initial preplanned one-on-one encounter—first date—usually requires the making of conversation. In a restaurant, the food that has been ordered (or may be ordered on a subsequent date) is usually a safe subject, but some communicators—wherever they are and whatever they're up to—can't stop themselves from making more adventurous forays.

"I love cabbage."
"Yeah, cabbage is awesome."

Heart-to-heart between admirers of slaw, in suburban restaurant.

"What's your favorite kind of *lunch meat?*"

Curious carnivore, at continental-style restaurant.

"I mean, **I like boobs,** but those shoes are fabulous."

Well-groomed man to woman, in redeveloped neighborhood.

"Oh, she **loves** people, especially gay men."

Woman to another, in dog park.

"Well, he's a convicted drunk driver, and she's a manicurist."

Career analyst, at a ski-resort restaurant.

"So we went back to my place. Guess who passed out again? Yep. Me."

Young woman on cell phone,
in town where people stay up late studying.

"I could pass the bar on a line of meth and no cigarettes." **"You're beautiful."**

*Shirtless, leather-vested man
and female admirer, in resort town.*

"Oh, my God!
Are you a Republican?
I mean, if you are, it's OK;
you can trust me."

*One undergraduate to another,
near campus arts center.*

53

"When I'm in love,
I gain weight,
like three or four
pounds.
So, we have to be careful."

*Woman to man, in
restaurant in tourist area.*

54

"There won't be a second date. *That girl ate way too many noodles.*"

Man cautious about carbs, surrounded by office towers.

"The date wasn't going well anyway. Then I look down and see **she's wearing a toe ring.**"

Man in suit and tie to man in suit and tie, near financial center.

"My blind date was a complete **waste of cleavage.**"

Over-baring woman, at bar in ritzy neighborhood.

"He's too old for me! I told you I needed arm candy, not an arm raisin."

Young woman to young woman, in theater ladies' room.

"What do you think of my date?"
"He's nice."
"Come on, what do you really think?"
"He's a little old for you, don't you think?"
"Oh, that's OK, because he's very immature."

Women discussing the age of reason, in café ladies' room.

Getting It *On*

If all systems are go, the first date could lead to the earth moving. Sex can be a shortcut to getting acquainted, making talk unnecessary, except for the boasting (and hashing and rehashing) that may follow.

> "So you called to tell me you don't feel like talking?"
>
> *Woman on cell phone, in market.*

> "We're doing *combat kissing* in the morning."
>
> *Young woman to pal, in neighborhood with many fusion restaurants.*

"It was really weird. First time I ever had sex with a *postmenopausal* woman."

Middle-aged man to another, in Italian restaurant.

"She *loves*
sex in the
but she
have a
in

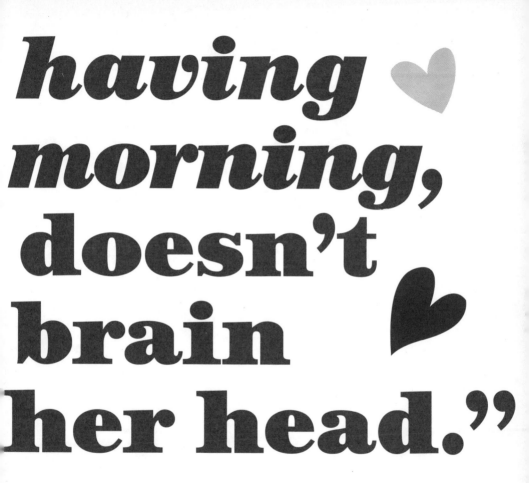

having ♥ *morning, doesn't brain her head."*

Gent to gent, on commuter ferry.

63

"Does he have *a pumice?*"

Woman to woman, at gardening store.

"I used to have that problem, until my *dance lessons* started to pay off."

Student of rhythm, in office complex.

"I aced Human Sexuality, **but I could have *taught* the course.**"

Self-assured scholar, at state college campus.

"What is it with women and that ***position?*** I get a lot of requests for it."

Man to group of women, in library café.

> "As soon as she gets out of bed to go to the bathroom, I'm out of there. **I don't want to get stabbed by some guy with a knife.**"

Wary man, at Mexican restaurant.

"No, I don't want sex today. I had sex *yesterday*. OK, here's my stop."

Woman with good memory,
aboard bus . . .

"It was very orgy-esque . . . but it was fun!"

Adventurous woman,
on hip shopping street.

"She told me I was *deceptively* clean-cut."

Well-groomed man, at waterfront bar.

"I used to think about it all the time. But now I'm thinking about *not thinking about it at all."*

Contemplating abstinence, on progressive campus.

"Helen, are you *lubricating?*"

Man to woman, in college music department.

Getting Techni-
cal

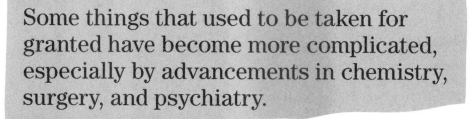

Some things that used to be taken for granted have become more complicated, especially by advancements in chemistry, surgery, and psychiatry.

"She must know I'm taking ***Viagra.*** What I'm doing is biologically impossible."

Realist, on hiking trail.

"So, are you still a **homosexual?** It can't hurt to check."

Uncompromising man, on shuttle to gay neighborhood.

"What **gender** do you consider yourself to be?"

Man conducting sidewalk survey, in neighborhood with many stores selling chaps and leashes.

"I used to date an **FTM**; now I'm dating an **MTF**. I'm all over the place."

Chitchat at urban hair salon.

"He can't be that gay; he got me pregnant."

Woman to woman, on university campus.

"He does know you're a lesbian, right?"

Advocate of full disclosure, at department store entrance.

"How can you be gay for a day?
If you're gay, you're gay."

Uncompromising man, near office buildings.

"She wasn't a radical lesbian
when she was married to
your father."

Woman with long memory, in restaurant.

"I told you to
never call me 'Sheila'
at the gym."

Man to man, in health-club locker room.

"Call Emily and me when
you lose your inhibitions."

Young woman to male friend, outside café.

"We are trying to work it out, but he refuses to give up the cross-dressing."

Woman to chum, during lunch break.

Abundant varieties of sexual opportunity can lead to high expectations, but many seekers of bliss are realistic. Shadows fall.

"She said I'm no good in bed, so I think I'm going to have to start channeling Barry White."

Man on cell phone, on shopping-district sidewalk.

"I don't care what you call me at home, as long as you say *I'm a man* in front of my friends."

Demander of respect, near convention center.

"There was the **standard drinking and flirting** and . . . a week or so later, I was taking antibiotics."

Consumer of prescription medicine, walking in city.

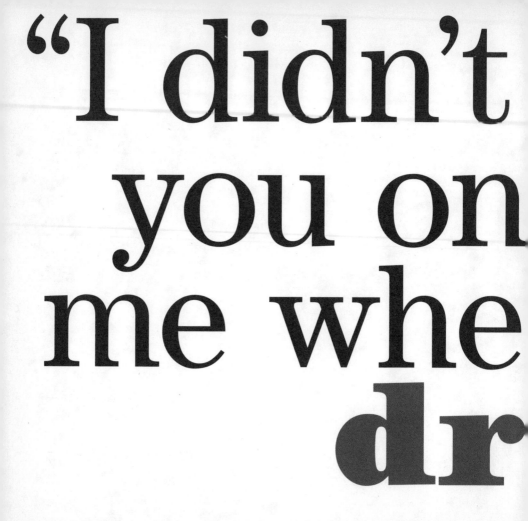

"I didn't
you on
me whe
dr

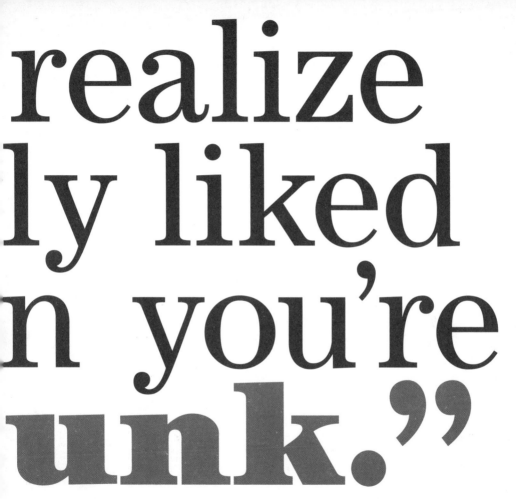

realize ly liked n you're unk."

Man on cell phone, at traffic-filled intersection.

"Don't **point** that thing at me."

Guest to another, at nightclub for players of sexual power games.

"It's not like we were saying **'chain your girlfriend to a boiling radiator'** or anything."

Gent describing his punk band to friends, at bar.

"Well, he doesn't usually *take off his boxers,* so it probably wasn't him."

Observant eyewitness, in stationery store.

"Sex on a *full* stomach is not so great. It's too hard to breathe."

Part-time gourmand, at cross-dressing-themed nightclub.

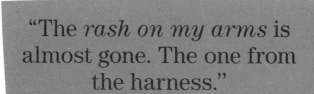

"The *rash on my arms* is almost gone. The one from the harness."

Tattooed woman in evening dress to dinner companions, at restaurant.

"With an Irish Catholic upbringing and my mother's influence, it was more *virginity* in life and wildness in the imagination."

Famous novelist-playwright, after performance of new drama.

"The penis isn't a brownie; *it's a macaroon.*"

Cookie-store counterperson to customer.

"My brother has a new girlfriend now. *She is already trying to Queer Eye him.*"

Woman having her locks coiffed, to hairdresser.

"You can never have sushi with a **metrosexual** because he always 'just had' sushi."

Woman to friend, near waterfront.

"I'm not going to
tell you again:
*no way I'm
going to shave
my head.*"

*Woman to man,
in airport in Hawaii.*

"If he's not going
to shave his face,
*then I'm not going to
shave my legs.*"

*Woman to woman,
in shopping mall.*

"You **shaved** it?"

Woman on cell phone, near upscale suburban stores.

"But does it scream *'Have sex with me'?"*

Victoria's Secret shopper showing friend a pair of red-lace panties trimmed with feathers.

"And then *I realized that of course
I had seen him naked before.*
We had walked five miles together
in the Bay to Breakers."

Veteran of cross-city athletic event.

"You are a pickle.
You'll never be a cucumber again."

*Woman to man, at bus terminal in
senior community.*

"I don't do adultery any more."

*One apartment dweller to another,
in high-rise for seniors.*

"There's got to be more kissing!
We need some tongue action. We don't want
to look like Stepford wives."

*Float captain to lesbian couple in Chinese
New Year parade.*

"Tonight we'll be taking a shower together.
Of course, it won't be as much
fun as it used to be."

Realistic resident of retirement home.

"So, that's two regular hookers and *four midgets.*"

Gents planning bachelor party,
at Mexican restaurant.

Getting

Realistic

Love may be many-splendored, but some people are annoying.

"He describes everything in his garden as the quintessential tomato or the quintessential squash. *I just don't think I'm quintessential enough for him.*"

Modest woman, at beach restaurant.

"I love you, but your credit's not that *good*."

*Man on cell phone,
at art exposition.*

"Yes, I watch hard-core porn. *Is that a problem?*"

Young woman on cell phone, in gardening store.

"What, you're going to have eggnog, and you won't let me have full-fat ice cream?"

Man to woman, at rural grocery store.

"Do you understand English?"
"You may be speaking English, but all I hear is 'me, me, me.'"

Man and woman, in martini bar.

"You made me feel *high-maintenance* when you moved the umbrella."

Woman to man, at brew pub.

"Why would I read your blog? I don't even like talking to you."

Woman on cell phone, in burrito shop.

"I told him **I won't sleep with him** until he takes veal off the menu."

Woman discussing restaurateur boyfriend with friend, in town where many people won't wear leather shoes.

"I told him, 'You will ***not* wear a *Speedo* in front of my family.'"

Young woman to another, walking on beach.

115

"I'm afraid her husband was one of the **toxic** substances in her environment."

Woman to woman, in busy restaurant.

"I'm expecting my **ex-wife** to visit at the end of the month, and then my **ex-husband** to visit the first of next month."

Man to man, in diverse neighborhood.

"**Women are *awful*.**

There have been studies done."

Man to man, at Starbucks.

"Dude, I told you it would be a *chick flick.* It's got 'Sisterhood' in the title."

Man to man, in town known for the study of gender issues.

"She knows that she can sleep with men **out of her league,** but she can't marry men out of her league."

Analytic observer, strolling through urban park.

"First wives are difficult."

Veteran shares his wisdom, over breakfast at high-tech café.

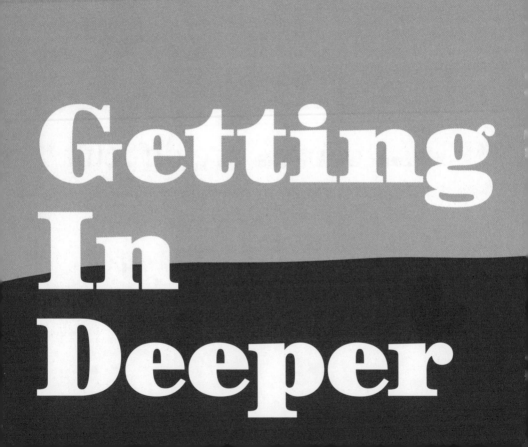

Getting In Deeper

If a person is lucky, at least once in a lifetime, love will reach full bloom. This is the stage when a man will quote his significant other's opinion on the death penalty or shag carpeting.

"She's gross. He's gross. They're both gross. *It's a good couple.*"

Young woman to young woman, at gaming table.

"I said I love you and think I want to spend my life with you, but right now I'm in Safeway and I can't find anything, **so I'll call you *later*."**

Older man on cell phone, surveying aisles.

"You call it **making _love._**
What does he call it?"

_Question of semantics,
posed on public transportation._

"That chicken
is my **soul mate."**

_Female friend of the feathered,
at panini restaurant._

> "If we get separated, let's meet at the charity **spanking booth.**"

One leather-clad gent to another, at S&M-oriented street fair.

Getting One's

Money's Worth

Couples must realize the effect of tangible goods on the romantic picture.

"Would you pick out **a nice avocado?** It's for someone very special to me."

Young man to supermarket produce clerk.

"My girlfriend is a clown. Do you have anything I can get her for her birthday?"

Customer to salesperson, at museum gift shop.

"What do you mean 'find one'? You *are* my **sugar daddy.**"

Woman to man,
at Chanel in Las Vegas.

"He's your husband;
just take the money.
It's part of the deal."

*Friend dispensing financial counsel,
on boutique-shopping street.*

"He won't date anyone
before Christmas.
**That way he doesn't
have to buy her a
present.**"

Fan to fan, at hockey game.

"I only open the **checks** and the **love letters.**"

One woman to another, in line at rural post office.

"I can't believe you pay for sex but you think popcorn is too *expensive.*"

Movie-lover to movie-lover, at multiplex cinema.

"You've just invoked your **'you only live once'** clause."

Man to woman, emerging from jewelry store.

Getting Advice

Some romantic paths are better left untrodden. The wise person recognizes a stop sign when he or she sees one.

"If my tongue wasn't down your throat, **it was *platonic*.**"

Woman on cell phone, in frozen-food section of supermarket.

"**I'm not partying with your girlfriend, *Dad*.** I don't care what you say."

Young woman on cell phone, at community college.

"I'm *obviously* trying to point out that the cat was, like, his boyfriend."

Man on cell phone, in discount grocery store.

"It would have been better if she had said **at the outset that she was forty,** instead of waiting a year."

"It didn't work out because
(a) he's thirty-nine years old,
(b) it was Friday night, and
(c) his mom was with him."

"I don't understand how the **bastard could marry** outside of his political persuasion."

Woman to man, near baseball stadium.

"I don't know why she would spend so much money on her second wedding."

Woman in business suit, cell phone in one hand, latte in another, on city street.

"She always marries the wrong man, but she does divorce so well."

Admiring observer, at Mediterranean restaurant.

"If you think you've **got to call the cops when you're going to break up with her,** I'd say it's time to take a look at your relationship."

Concerned adviser to young man, in hospital elevator.

"When he wanted to slit my throat,
I didn't care what his feelings were."
"He flies off the handle,
and then you have to live with him."

Two men in conversation, aboard bus.

"I kind of got turned off

when my psychic started *stalking* me."

Woman to pals, at urban café.

"He said he shaped it like a steak and
fed it to his partner,
and she didn't know the difference."

Man on cell phone, in budget supermarket.

Getting
Hitched

It's not out of style to get married, a ritual that can have philosophical and practical complications.

"That's my problem: always a bride and *never a bridesmaid*."

One matron to another, in verdant suburb.

"I think he married the first **nonhooker** he met."

Man on cell phone, on commuter train.

"The honeymoon was great, but it got a little weird with all her uncles."

Man to man, at Japanese restaurant.

"I knew I was in trouble when she boosted up the date of the wedding to coincide with her mother's birthday."

Man with foresight, at chain Italian restaurant.

"The thing about a **wedding cake** is that it has to be structurally sound."

Constructivist woman, hiking in park.

"When the **best man's Chewbacca,** that's bad."

Woman analyzing wedding with a Star Wars theme.

"She wants to get married at Shakespeare Garden, but I really **want my dog to be there.**"

Promoter of inclusivity, on streetcar headed downtown.

"This is the perfect wedding ring.
It fits just great under my cycling gloves."

Newlywed cycling enthusiast to office mates.

"I don't care whose wedding it is; I'm not **wearing a dickey.**"

Young man, leaving vintage clothing store.

"The bride is my cousin, **my cousin twice *removed*, actually.** And, might I add, twice removed for a reason."

Pessimist to listener, at wine-country wedding reception.

"I got her and Ken some wonderful gifts. They better stay together."

Contemplating the future, at art deco exhibit.

Getting Relief

Outside assistance is sometimes available, but whether it helps is debatable.

"So, I guess I should tell you, **I *slept* with your sister** while you were gone."

Man on cell phone, in front of Macy's.

"It was an amazing coincidence that the ***sermon was about adultery.***"

Worshipful woman, in waterfront town.

"Didn't you know I was having an affair with my boss? After all, we work together, **so it's not like I'm *screwing* every Tom, Dick, and Harry.**"

Woman to friend, browsing in bookstore.

"No, no, no, I wasn't *embezzling.* I was having an affair."

Man to friends, at innovative restaurant.

"She only *broke off the affair* with a married man when she found out he was carrying on another affair with her cousin, a man."

Woman to another, at fund-raiser for homeless shelter.

"I need two exactly the same, **so that when I talk to each of them,** I'll be able to keep it straight."

Man shopping for valentines, to clerk.

Getting

Out

Exit strategies are often considered and sometimes deployed.

"Here's a story about a man **who committed his wife** to the *Humane Society*."

Woman reading magazine aloud to man.

"I already **killed my husband** doing the rug thing."

Wife who either poisoned her husband with fumes from cleaning chemicals, pushed his back out with sex on the floor, or shamed him by making him wear a toupee.

"It wasn't about the **torture;** it was about the fact that **I'm going to be *allergic* to you.**"

Man at medical center, in need of international intervention or antihistamines.

> **"My boyfriend is so nice,** I can't figure out how to break up with him. *Maybe I will just start dating women."*

Woman, at restaurant.

"Whoever divorced her made the right decision."

Man appraising sour-faced woman, at gala.

"Your wife is not entirely wrong. Dead is dead."

Man taken into confidence, on street lined with boutiques.

"I hate it when a **self-fulfilling prophecy** comes true."

Woman to friend, in downtown plaza.

"He put a *spell* on me, and that was, like, so inappropriate."

One receptionist to another, behind waiting-room desk.

"And I got to say to my daughter,
'Yeah, that's your father. He's *ugly*.'
And all the people at the one-hour photo got
to see my boobs and my butt."

Woman to woman, in pasta restaurant.

"You didn't meet his expectations,
and you were gone. He was almost the
Simon Cowell of dating."

Woman hiking on trail, in hilly park.

"She is my second wife. I'm actually much closer to my first wife, though. **We've exchanged gunfire.**"

Man remembering the happy times, at diner.

"Mommy isn't allowed
to carry a knife, and for a
very good reason."

Woman to child, on bus.

"I am a barnacle on your
family's **tuchus.**"

*Younger woman to older woman,
in line at coffeehouse.*

"She left me.
Now I'm dating our goldfish."

Man to pal, at farmers' market.

"What was kind of weird was you called to ask me if you could come by to pick up the **Viagra** so you could have sex with someone else."

Young woman on cell phone, on bus.

"I wouldn't marry him— *he's a dick*— but I was very flattered to be asked."

Woman on cell phone, at art show.

"Today was a breast day.
Tomorrow might be a wing day. It's just the way it is."

Counterperson at KFC, perhaps discussing the fickle nature of love.

"I'm the person who talks you through these *horrible* situations! I'm the person who's been by your side through *major* life events!"

*Man on cell phone set to speaker mode,
on major shopping street.*

"And he said, 'I knew it—
not all miracles are true!'
and he threw his peanut butter and
jelly sandwich at me."

*Woman to man,
walking near stock exchange.*

"Tell her to let it go, it's over,
time to move on."
"But she keeps *barking* all night."

*Man to man, on commercial street
in singles neighborhood.*

"I just called to tell
you we're not an **item**
anymore."

Man on cell phone, near chain coffeehouse.

"If it has **tires** or *testicles*, it's going to be trouble."

Woman to woman, over lunch at Neiman Marcus.

"So I said to her, 'Lady, the one thing **I can't change** is your husband's face.'"

Man on cell phone, near convention center.

Getting
Senti

mental

Most people savor memories.

"I didn't think I was married, but I *am* married."

Woman on cell phone, in working-class community.

"With all the money I will be getting from this, I am thinking maybe I will **remarry my ex-wife.**"

Nostalgic guy, hiking near redwoods.

"I made a special dinner last night. **I thought of you** while using the little grinder."

Woman on cell phone, in mega–chain supermarket in suburb.

> "Oh, they're not **divorcing** each other. They're **divorcing** their marriage."
>
> *Woman to woman, outside an Old Navy.*

"We were in the process of breaking up, but **I couldn't figure out** how much of me was leaving with him."

Woman having trouble with calculations, at art-auction fund-raiser.

> "It just doesn't seem right to be here in **San Francisco** and not be with you. I just had to call."

*Woman on cell phone,
in line at natural grocery store.*

Getting There

Some couples *actually* survive.

"I have really **low standards,**
so it works out just fine."

Man to woman, in pizzeria.

"Three little kids and
***happily* married.**
I don't know what there is to be
so depressed about."

Teenager to mother, at shopping center.

"You don't have a female side.
Your wife is your female side. **Duh.**"

One gent to another, near giant record store.

"Remind me if **I know anybody.**"

Middle-aged man to woman, entering restaurant.

"I know she is **ovulating** right now."

Man on cell phone, in upscale supermarket.

"She cooked it. **I ate it.** That was forty years ago."

Man to another, in bar in Italian neighborhood.

"And that's why **I'm pregnant.**"

*One woman to another, emerging from elevator
in state office building.*

Acknowledgments

A writer of memoirs once said that each person is the author of his or her own story. So, to you who have spoken without being aware that an outsider was listening, thank you for your literary contributions. Keep on talking, and don't worry if people are eavesdropping. In fact, you might ramp up the volume a bit for the audience's benefit.

Thank you, too, to each person who submitted quotes. For the future, please practice scribbling legibly without breaking your stride. You hear some of the best things while walking on the street.

Here at the *San Francisco Chronicle*, thank you to Wendy Miller, wise editor and terrific all-around pal, and Phil Bronstein, who supported the concept from its first whisper. And thanks to neighbors at nearby desks, who have had to put up with my whooping, hollering, and reading aloud treasured e-mails.

Most important, thanks to Jerry for years of conversation, spoken and not, while on the run from Brooklyn.